Choose Your Weapon:
Combined Operational Effectiveness and Investment Appraisal (COEIA) and its Role in UK Defence Procurement

David Kirkpatrick

Royal United Services Institute for Defence Studies

First Published 1996

© Royal United Services Institute for Defence Studies

All rights reserved. No part of this publication may be reproduced, stored in a retrieval system, or transmitted in any form or by any means, electronic, mechanical, photocopying, recording or otherwise, without prior permission of the Royal United Services Institute for Defence Studies.

ISBN 0-85516-135-3
ISSN 0268-1307

The Royal United Services Institute for Defence Studies (RUSI) is a professional body based in London dedicated to the study, analysis and debate of issues affecting defence and international security.

Founded in 1831 by the Duke of Wellington, the RUSI is one of the most senior institutes of its kind in the world which, throughout its history, has been at the forefront of contemporary political-military thinking through debates, public and private seminars, conferences, lectures and a wide range of publications. The independence of the Institute is guaranteed by a large, worldwide membership of those people and organisations who have a serious and professional interest in the thorough and objective analysis of defence and international security.

Critical and acclaimed analysis of issues of the moment has underwritten the RUSI's Whitehall Papers for many years. The new series will, in its revised A5 monograph format, continue to provide expertise in the field. The series, which will comprise six publications a year, will address the major areas of current interest.

Whitehall Papers are available as part of a membership package, or singly at £6.50 plus p & p (£1.00 in the UK/ £2.00 overseas). Orders should be sent to the Publications Department, RUSI, Whitehall, London SW1A 2ET and cheques and postal orders made payable to the RUSI.

Printed in Great Britain by Sherrens Printers, Units 1 & 2, South Park, Granby Industrial Estate, Weymouth, Dorset.
The Royal United Services Institute for Defence Studies, Whitehall, London SW1A 2ET.
Registered Charity No. 210639

CONTENTS

Introduction		1
Chapter 1	Background	4
Chapter 2	Formulation of Requirements	12
Chapter 3	COEIA—Concept of Analysis	16
Chapter 4	Investment Appraisal	22
Chapter 5	Operational Effectiveness	32
Chapter 6	Synthesis and Presentation of Results	38
Chapter 7	Applications	45
Chapter 8	Further Developments?	50
Chapter 9	The Way Ahead	55
Chapter 10	Conclusion	59
Annex A		60
Annex B		64

PREFACE

The Royal United Services Institute for Defence Studies invited me to write this paper, drawing on my many years experience of the United Kingdom Ministry of Defence. Most recently, as Director of Project Time and Cost Analysis in the Controllerate of Aircraft, I participated in several major Combined Operational Effectiveness and Investment Appraisal (COEIA) studies contributing to UK procurement decisions on fighter aircraft, medium support helicopters, attack helicopters and tactical transport aircraft. This paper reviews the new MoD procedure for COEIA studies and the role of these studies in MoD procurement of defence equipment, and discusses some possible developments in that procedure. The paper has benefited from the constructive comments of my colleagues (past and present), but the views expressed in it are mine and mine alone. I am grateful to the Institute for the invitation to help disseminate a better understanding of the scope and objectives of COEIA studies.

BIOGRAPHICAL NOTE

Dr David Kirkpatrick has worked on aerodynamics research in the Royal Aircraft Establishment at Farnborough, on military operational analysis in the Ministry of Defence, and on life cycle cost analysis and forecasting in the Procurement Executive. Since his retirement from the Ministry of Defence, he has become Senior Lecturer and Deputy Head of the Defence Engineering Group at University College London, and a Visiting Fellow at the University of York's Centre for Defence Economics.

INTRODUCTION

Few decisions are more important for the security of a nation state than the selection and procurement of weapon systems for its Armed Forces. In modern warfare even the bravest and most energetic troops, directed by the most skilful and judicious leaders, can rarely surmount the crippling handicap of being less well equipped than their enemy. In the Napoleonic period, when most of the weaponry of the opposing armies was virtually identical (smoothbore muskets and cannon for the infantry and artillery, sabres and lances for the cavalry), it was the numbers, training and motivation of the troops as well as the talents of their commanders which were decisive. At that time, 'God was on the side of the big battalions'.[1] In modern times developments in technology have stimulated rapid advance in the capabilities of weapon systems, and those forces which have been equipped with the heavier artillery, more-powerful armoured fighting vehicles (AFV), more-capable torpedoes and more-agile fighter aircraft have generally been victorious in combat. Training, motivation and leadership remain important (since inexperienced or disloyal troops and incompetent or unlucky leaders can incur disaster even when well equipped), but when the opposing forces are similarly endowed with these qualities, it is the relative performance of their weapon systems which is decisive and numbers are now less important.

The selection and procurement of weapon systems for a nation's Armed Forces has always been a difficult and challenging task. In war the penalties of failure can inflict death, wounds or captivity on an ill-equipped Serviceman, disgrace on his commander, and capitulation on his defeated nation. In peacetime the penalties of error in defence procurement are less dramatic, but the guilty officers and officials may be severely criticised by government committees[2] and their careers may be irrevocably blighted; the more-serious effects of such errors are the risks from ill-designed or unreliable equipment to Servicemen in training, and potential public disenchantment with defence expenditure which may reduce the funds available below the level necessary for national security. Since the Second World War the task of selection and procure-

Choose Your Weapon

ment has become more difficult as developments in military technology have presented a cornucopia of alternative weapon systems and concepts which, when properly exploited by the appropriate strategy and tactics, have yielded a succession of transformations in modern warfare.[3] The task has also become more difficult because of the long timescales required for the development of modern complex weapon systems, and the associated problem of predicting the policies and capabilities of potentially hostile nations some decades in the future.

Different nations approach the selection of defence equipment in different ways depending on the scale of each nation's defence budget, the diversity of its global responsibilities, and the capabilities of its defence industrial base. This paper describes the current UK procedures for equipment selection and approval for procurement, and in particular the new Combined Operational Effectiveness and Investment Appraisal (COEIA) procedure which has been adopted to assist the selection of defence equipment (both weapon systems and supporting systems). It must be emphasised that the COEIA procedure is concerned only with military and financial issues, and does not address issues of industrial and foreign policy which may contribute to UK government decisions on defence procurement. It should also be emphasised that the COEIA procedures are not entirely new—similar operational effectiveness studies were undertaken to support procurement of Tornado aircraft in the 1960s and investment appraisal techniques have been used for many years to evaluate alternative procurement options in MoD and other UK government departments—but they are now embodied in a formal requirement to ensure that all proposals for the procurement of defence equipment are supported by the same high standard of analysis of cost and effectiveness.

Notes

1. Voltaire *Lettres à M. Le Riche,* 6 February, 1770.
2. In the UK, defence procurement is overseen by the House of Common's Defence Select Committee and by the Public Accounts Committee. In the US, oversight is the responsibility of the Armed Services Committees of the House

Introduction

of Representatives and of the Senate.

3. Notable strategic transformations have been caused by nuclear, chemical and biological weapons, and at the tactical level by attack helicopters, precision-guided munitions, satellite-assisted navigation, stealth, and data processing.

CHAPTER 1
BACKGROUND

The Armed Forces of the UK have evolved to three Services—Royal Navy, Army and Royal Air Force—operating in the sea, land and air environments. Historically these Services have often disagreed over their respective responsibilities at the interfaces of these environments (amphibious troops, maritime air operations and tactical air support), but it is now recognised that in virtually all major future operations by UK Forces the sea, land and air elements of these forces will be interdependent. Accordingly in 1985 the Ministry of Defence (MoD) was reorganised[1] to create a tri-service Defence Staff responsible for all future planning of defence policy, operations and procurement. The Defence Staff now directs operational analysis of the future military operations which contribute to the agreed Defence Roles of UK forces, and also directs scientific research in key areas of defence technology to explore their potential and to identify possible problems. The operational analysis and the scientific research studies are generally undertaken on behalf of the MoD by the Centre for Defence Analysis (CDA) and the Defence Research Agency (DRA) respectively; both of these organisations are divisions of the Defence Evaluation and Research Agency (DERA) which was formed in 1995 to be the MoD's principal supplier of advice on defence technology and equipment. The Defence Staff uses the results of the operational analysis studies to establish the future need for a particular military capability, and uses the results of the scientific research to formulate a Staff Target, and subsequently a Staff Requirement, which define the qualities of new defence equipment which is needed to provide that military capability.

Within the Ministry of Defence, the Procurement Executive was established in 1971[2] to manage the procurement of defence equipment for all three Services, and lately for the tri-service Defence Staff, so that the equipment achieves the required performance, is delivered at the right time, and provides best value for money from the MoD budget. To fulfil

Background

that role the Procurement Executive maintains appropriate relationships with UK industry and with MoD research establishments. Before the COEIA procedure was introduced, the Procurement Executive used the investment appraisal procedures specified in the Treasury Guide[3]— 'Economic Appraisal in Central Government—A Technical Guide for Government Departments'—to compare alternative equipment options which met the particular Staff Requirement considered, and to assess different strategies for the procurement of each equipment option.

Consequently in the past the UK procedure for selection and procurement of military equipment tended to operate as a two-stage process, with specification and justification of the military operational requirement by the Defence Staff followed by identification and procurement by the Procurement Executive of the most economical equipment to meet that requirement (see Fig 1a). In theory there was scope for constructive interaction between the Defence Staff and the Procurement Executive, which might together consider the implications for equipment cost and effectiveness of the various specifications in a Staff Requirement. The standard language in every Staff Requirement specifically invited contractors to consider whether large reductions in cost could be achieved by modest easing of some of the Requirement's specifications. But in practice only the more enlightened officers and officials were able to establish a constructive dialogue, and frequently both the Defence Staffs and the Procurement Executive regarded the detailed provisions of a Staff Requirement as immutable (at least until economic realities insisted that a project was unaffordable). Too often, the Procurement Executive and the defence industry were reluctant to presume to debate Staff Requirements which the customer Services had already formulated and agreed, nor was the Defence Staff always particularly receptive to civilian meddling with the essential characteristics of the equipment which its own judgement had indicated were necessary to ensure victory.

This MoD procedure also produced chronic disagreements with the Treasury, which was always suspicious of a Service's unsupported military judgement that it really needed the sophisticated (and costly)

Choose Your Weapon

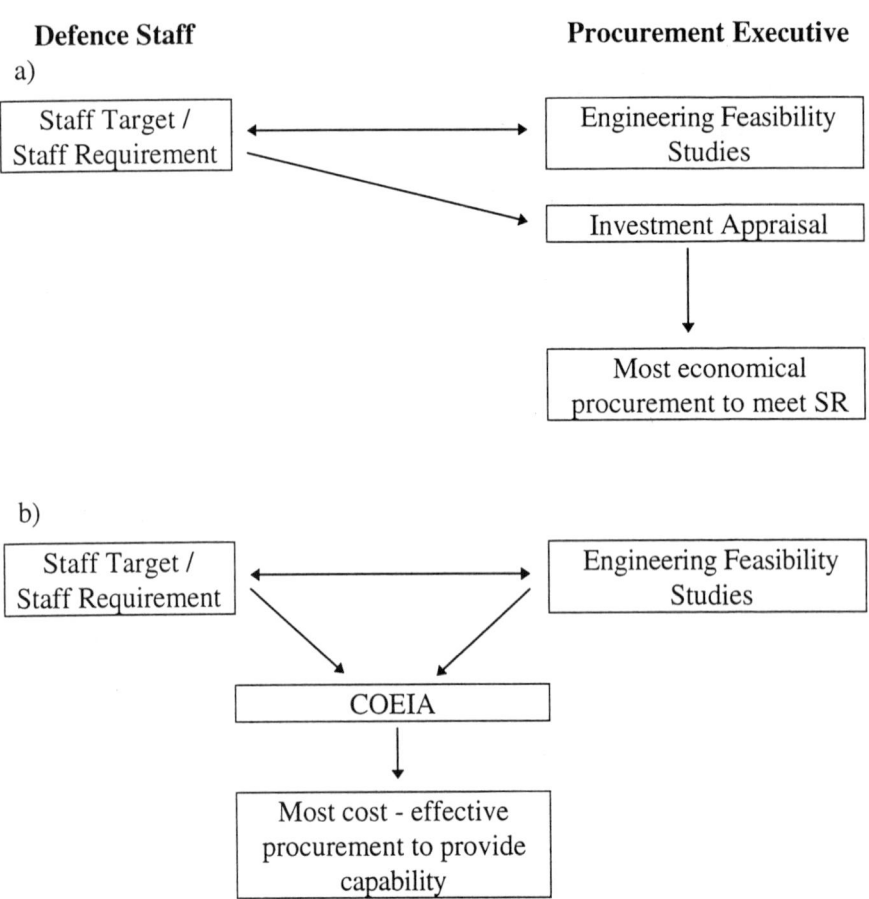

Fig 1. Former (a) and New (b) procurement processes.

Background

equipment which was specified in a Staff Requirement. Even when military judgement was assembled systematically to ensure an impartial consensus, and was supported by evidence from exercises or recent conflicts, the Treasury could not always be convinced that equipment procurements proposed by the MoD represented good value for money.

The Buckley Report and its consequences

A recent review of the UK equipment procurement procedures (the Buckley Report[4]) called for substantial changes to the decision-making machinery. In particular, it specified that future proposals for equipment procurement should be accompanied, *inter alia*, by a cost-effectiveness report based on the results of operational analysis and on forecasts of the life cycle cost of the alternative equipment options. The requirement for a cost-effectiveness report was prompted by the established procedure in the United States of requiring a Cost and Operational Effectiveness Analysis (COEA) to support key decisions by the Defence Acquisitions Board. However, UK plans for the adoption of cost-effectiveness studies into the procurement process had to take account of limitations on the human and financial resources which the MoD can apply to studies of cost and operational effectiveness, and of the existing Treasury Technical Guide specifying procedures for economic appraisal of public expenditure. Accordingly, MoD has chosen the title 'Combined Operational Effectiveness and Investment Appraisal' (COEIA) to emphasise that the UK was not adopting the COEIA process in its entirety, and that the Treasury's Technical Guide procedures remain in force.

MoD implementation of the Buckley recommendations established a small high-level Equipment Approvals Committee (EAC) and a set of internal MoD Guidelines[5] for preparation of the seven Dossier papers which contribute to EAC's decisions. The EAC has only four members (CSA, VCDS, CDP and 2nd PUS). Its Chairman is the Chief Scientific Adviser (CSA), who is normally a distinguished scientist on a short-term employment contract with the MoD and is therefore expected to surmount factional prejudice; his MoD staff are responsible for scrutiny of scientific, technical and risk aspects of all equipment projects for UK

Choose Your Weapon

forces, for advice on all aspects of the UK defence nuclear programme, for the proper application of analytical and quantitative methods to defence decision making, and for management of the MoD's Corporate Research Programme. The Vice Chief of the Defence Staff (VCDS) is the officer (soldier, sailor or airman) who leads all Service planning of operations, force development, equipment programmes, command/control/communications/information (C^3I) systems, logistics and personnel matters. The Chief of Defence Procurement (CDP) leads the Procurement Executive responsible for the efficient procurement of new equipment and mid-life updates. The 2nd Permanent Under Secretary (2nd PUS) is responsible for resources, programmes and finance (including management of the budget), MoD's infrastructure and its use of information technology, for the personnel management of MoD's civilian staff, and for the accounting, audit and analysis of the MoD's budget.[6] These four members, therefore, cover all the main areas of defence policy which relate to decisions on defence procurement. The seven papers which form a Dossier are:

1. *Covering Paper*, describing briefly the equipment programme and the issues associated with it; this Paper should present to the EAC their staffs' conclusions and recommendations, noting particularly the trade-off between alternatives and any uncertainties and policy issues which could influence decision-making;

2. *Requirement Definition*, presenting and justifying the operational requirement, and the alternative ways of meeting it; this Paper may refer to a Staff Target/Staff Requirement accompanying the Dossier;

3. *Combined Operational Effectiveness and Investment Appraisal*, presenting forecasts of the relative operational effectiveness and life cycle cost of all the practicable alternative equipment options, and fully describing the main features of the Operational Effectiveness and Investment Appraisal studies; this Paper may refer to detailed information (e.g. on scenarios, specifications and methodology) in other reports which do not accompany the Dossier but are available to the EAC's staff if required;

Background

4. *Procurement Issues and Strategy,* covering for each of the alternative equipment options the plans for its procurement from the relevant contractor, the progress of any relevant technology demonstrators or trials, plans for the assessment and management of technical and other risks, intended arrangements for contracting and acceptance into service, as well as the consequences of selecting that option for UK industry, balance of trade, foreign policy and the environment;

5. *Programme Baseline,* listing the principal operational characteristics of the military requirement and the intended schedule for development, production and delivery of new equipment, and comparing the profile of forecast annual expenditure on procurement, operations and support of the favoured equipment option(s) with the MoD's budgetary provision for the project; the total life cycle cost of the project and the cost of its major phases must be expressed as three-point estimates, citing the Expected Cost and the Upper and Lower Costs (such that the actual cost is very unlikely to fall outside the range they define), and presented in a Project Costing Certificate signed by the Project Director, who thereby assumes responsibility for their accuracy;

6. *Support Strategy,* covering the logistic aspects of the alternative equipment options, including consideration of the scale of Service manpower required and the complexity of their tasks;

7. *Project Validity and Affordability Statement,* compiled by the Resources and Programmes Staff taking account of other demands on the defence budget.

The new procurement process (based on the requirements of COEIA and the other Dossier papers) is now more integrated, with the Defence Staff and the Procurement Executive working closely together to identify the most cost-effective procurement of equipment to provide a required military capability (see Fig 1b). In this new process a COEIA should be undertaken in support of each EAC decision to allocate substantial funds to the next stage of a project's procurement. Defence equipment for the MoD can pass through up to seven stages in its life cycle[7]—Concept, Feasibility Study, Project Definition, Full Development, System Production, In-service and Disposal—but if the equipment is procured off the shelf, only the last three stages are relevant. If the equipment considered is expected to follow Downey procedures[8] through all seven stages, a COEIA concept of analysis, defining the scope and methodology of the first COEIA to address this equipment project, should be produced before the start of the Feasibility Study (which is intended to establish the technical feasibility of the project and to provide initial forecasts of its performance cost and timescale). The first COEIA should be done during the Feasibility Study so that its results are available to obtain approval for funding to cover Project Definition (which develops a technical specification of the project's design and performance characteristics, formulates plans for later stages of procurement, defines and reduces any technical risks, and provides definitive forecasts of project cost and timescale). A more detailed and definitive COEIA should then be prepared to justify approval of funding for Full Development, and subsequently another to justify approval for System Production. Because the new procedure has been introduced into an ongoing defence equipment procurement programme, there are at present many projects for which COEIA are being done for the first time to support decisions on Full Development or System Production. However, if it is planned that the equipment considered would be bought off the shelf, the first and only COEIA would be required when seeking approval for procurement, in parallel to the tender assessment process.

Notes

1. *The Central Organisation for Defence* (Cmnd 9315), (HMSO, London, July 1985).
2. *Government Organisation for Defence Procurement and Civil Aerospace* (Cmnd 4641), (HMSO, London, April 1971).
3. HM Treasury, *Economic Appraisal in Central Government—A Technical Guide for Government Departments*, (HMSO, London, 1991).
4. *Report of the EPC Efficiency Scrutiny*, unpublished MoD report, 17 May 1991.

Background

5. *Equipment Approvals Committee (EAC), Guidelines for the Dossier System*, unpublished MoD report, August 1994.

6. *Stable Forces in a Strong Britain*, Statement on the Defence Estimates, (HMSO, London, May 1995) shows that the MoD budget of £22 billion in financial year 1994-95 supported 256 000 Service personnel and 139 000 civilians.

7. *Britain's Defence Procurement*, Defence Public Relations (E & P) MoD, 1993.

8. *Report of a Steering Group on Development Cost Estimating*, (HMSO, London, 1969) presents the Downey procedures for project management, which stipulate that each stage in a project's life cycle must be satisfactorily completed before the next is begun, and that sufficient scientific and engineering work must be done in the first three stages to allow full development to be undertaken with confidence that satisfactory values of the project's performance, cost and timescale will be achieved.

CHAPTER 2
FORMULATION OF REQUIREMENT

Before considering the various aspects of the COEIA procedure in more detail, it is important to emphasise that the COEIA procedure is intended to *support the selection from alternative options of defence equipment to satisfy a justified military operational requirement.* It follows that a COEIA should be preceded by high-level studies to determine the force mix which could most economically undertake the future military tasks of UK forces.

The structure of UK Armed Forces is designed to provide the necessary military capability to undertake the set of three Defence Roles (DR) which have been specified as the foundation of British defence and security policy. These Defence Roles are:

DR1—to ensure the protection and security of the United Kingdom and its Dependent Territories, even when there is no external threat;
DR2—to insure against a major external threat to the United Kingdom and its allies;
DR3—to contribute to promoting the United Kingdom's wider security interests through the maintenance of international peace and stability.

These Roles are subdivided into 50 Military Tasks, which the Armed Forces must be organised, trained and equipped to undertake successfully. Having identified the Tasks, the MoD must then determine how they can be accomplished and what equipment would be required. Concepts of operation are developed to define how the Tasks may best be performed, and force-mix studies (also called resource-allocation studies) are made to identify the most cost-effective mix of equipment to provide the necessary capabilities in future years.

To identify the most cost-effective future force mix, and hence the most effective programme of expenditure from the UK's future defence

Formulation of Requirements

budgets, military operational analyses at the Centre for Defence Analysis use MoD-approved scenarios and concepts of operation to consider the different increments to force cost and effectiveness which would result from the procurement and operation in service of various numbers of different classes of equipment to supplement or replace the existing national inventory. These studies should cover all classes of equipment which might be effective in future military tasks, using for each class generic forecasts of its cost and performance (and hence of its effectiveness in the approved scenarios). It is important that the operational analysis studies should adequately represent all significant features of military operations, including those features such as electronic warfare, command & control and operational degradation which are more difficult to model than ballistics and terrain screening. Since studies can rarely represent *all* relevant operational factors with complete confidence, any deficiencies in the models should be clearly identified and the studies' results should be interpreted with appropriate scientific and military judgement. It is also important that the scenarios used for force-mix studies should be comprehensive, and that they do not inadvertently incorporate any features which favour one class of equipment relative to another.

In principle it might be possible for an extensive programme of operational analysis studies to suggest the optimal balance of investment in various classes of equipment to maximise the effectiveness of UK forces in a given scenario. The same process, on an even larger scale, could suggest the optimal force mix to operate in a set of alternative scenarios. Any class of equipment would be included in the optimal force mix (for example, anti-tank helicopters would be included in the force mix to withstand enemy armoured forces) only if its generic unit cost and unit effectiveness in the approved scenarios are sufficiently attractive—i.e. if investment in this class of equipment increases the effectiveness of UK forces more than similar investment in another class. Once a particular class of equipment is established in the optimal force mix, the number of units of that class to be procured may be determined by balancing that number with the numbers of other equipments in the force in order to maximise its overall cost-effectiveness, within the constraints of viable operational and command structures. The high-level studies therefore establish and justify the need for a particular class of equipment to fulfil the future operational objectives of UK forces, and also suggest the number of each class which should be procured. Such studies are sometimes called 'needs and numbers' studies.

But the rigorous optimisation process outlined in the preceding paragraph is not always possible, and even where possible it is not always justifiable. Such optimisation would demand a large number of operational analysis studies (using models or simulations as appropriate) to cover the multitude of possible force mixes, and even more studies to allow for the tactical interdependence of the effectiveness of different classes of equipment. Furthermore the optimal force mix thus derived from a protracted and expensive programme of studies would not be robust because of the approximations and uncertainties inherent in military operation analysis at campaign level, and because of uncertainty in the postulated cost and effectiveness of future equipment. In practice, analysts select with military advice a set of candidate force mixes, each containing different numbers of different classes of equipment chosen so that the numbers are operationally plausible and so that the total cost of the force mix is close to a target budget. The effectiveness of each force mix can then be calculated and compared. From the results, it is possible to suggest which classes of equipment should be included in the force mix, to indicate the numbers of each class which would be required, and to provide guidelines on the desirable cost and effectiveness characteristics which can form the basis of a Staff Requirement for that class. Such calculations could be repeated for other budget levels to illustrate whether the results are sensitive to the future budget available.

The results of 'needs and numbers' studies must depend on the future military tasks envisaged for UK Forces (acting either independently or as a part of an allied force), on the level of effectiveness to be achieved by UK Forces, and on the limits of the British defence budget. Thus a change in the threat to UK, such as the collapse of the military power of the Warsaw Pact, should affect not only the scale but also the composition of future UK Forces. The 'needs and numbers' studies use representative

Formulation of Requirements

projections of the future threat and of future military tasks to justify the need for a particular class of military system, and hence for the issue of a Request for Proposals to UK and other contractors capable of supplying to the MoD alternative equipments in that class. The MoD must then select the equipment offering best value for money, and the COEIA procedure (described in the following chapters) is designed to assist that selection.

CHAPTER 3
COEIA —A CONCEPT OF ANALYSIS

The first stage in any COEIA must be the formulation of a concept of analysis and its approval by the appropriate MoD branches. The concept of analysis must refer to the relevant force-mix studies (see Chapter 2) which have provided justification for the procurement of a particular class of equipment, and which have indicated in general terms the number and performance of such equipment which should be provided for UK forces. The concept of analysis must then set out the alternative equipment options (from within that class) to be considered in the COEIA, the assumed procurement and support strategy for each option, the MoD-approved scenarios and concepts of operation within which the operational effectiveness of each equipment option will be evaluated, and the method of presentation of the final results. In all cases, the concept of analysis must be approved by the Chief Scientist (formerly the Deputy Chief Scientific Advisor) and the Assistant Under Secretary (Systems) or their staffs, depending on the scale and significance of the project. For major projects the approval of HM Treasury is also obtained, to preclude later disagreement at Cabinet level over the conduct of the COEIA and hence dissent about its conclusions.

Range of alternatives

The range of equipment considered in the COEIA should include all practicable alternatives from the list below:

    a) continue to operate existing equipment, with only normal maintenance and repair;
    b) continue to operate existing equipment with normal maintenance and repair, and with refurbishment when necessary to extend the equipment's service life without changing its performance;
    c) procure or lease replacement equipment (new or second-hand) with broadly the same capability as the existing equipment but

capable of operation over a longer period;
d) upgrade existing equipment to enhance its capability, generally in association with refurbishment to extend its service life;
e) procure or lease off-the-shelf equipment (new or second-hand) with superior performance and other qualities relative to the existing equipment;
f) promote and fund the development and production of new equipment to meet the relevant Staff Requirement.

Option a. is a 'do-nothing' option, which is associated with an inadequate and diminishing level of operational effectiveness in future years, but which must be included in all cases to form a datum from which increases in military capability and funding may be measured. Option d. may include several sub-options, covering a range of permutations of different levels of enhancement of the various subsystems incorporated in the existing equipment, applied to all or to a proportion of the current inventory. Options e. and f. may also include many sub-options covering different designs of equipment at various stages of development in UK and abroad, and a range of procurement and support strategies in each case. Options b. and c. generally fall short of the performance specified in the Staff Requirement, but options d., e. and f. may either match, exceed or fall short of that specification; option f. would be designed to meet the Staff Requirement as closely as is technically practicable, falling short only where the development process reveals that meeting the original specification would be unjustifiably expensive and exceeding the specification only where this involves negligible additional costs. Any of these options might involve private venture funding arrangements, by which industry would provide some or all of the investment needed to demonstrate new technology and to develop equipment suitable for the MoD and for other potential military or civil customers. The COEIA options may include a homogenous fleet of multi-role equipment with a design capable of undertaking all the military tasks cited in the Staff Requirement, and a heterogeneous fleet of two or more specialist equipments whose designs each provide limited but complementary capabilities. The range of options chosen for the COEIA must include all practicable options which might offer best value for money, without including too many to be adequately assessed by the MoD's limited analytical resources.

Scenario and operational concept

The concept of analysis must also define the scenario(s) and operational concept(s) within which the alternative equipment options will be assessed. Since prediction of potential operations by UK forces some decades in the future is a very inexact science, the chosen scenarios are intended to be representative of likely future operations rather than forecasts of actual operations which are expected to occur. It is inferred that the ranking of the alternative equipment options from assessment of their effectiveness in the chosen scenario(s) would be reflected by their ranking in actual operations. Each representative scenario must define (in sufficient detail for assessment) the objectives of UK forces, the enemy and allied units involved, and the climate, terrain, visibility, sea conditions etc. in the area of operations.

Measures of effectiveness

The result of the COEIA may be determined by its choice of one or more measures of equipment effectiveness, such as the number of enemy AFV destroyed or the delay imposed on an enemy advance, or the tonnage of supplies delivered to a forward area. These measures must be specified *in advance* of the COEIA analysis, to ensure that the analysis devotes sufficient attention to those operational features which are relevant to the chosen measure(s) of effectiveness. It is logical to follow the MoD's traditional policy of measuring the benefits of new military equipment in terms of its effectiveness in a future conflict—that is, in terms of the probability of victory to UK and its allies in the agreed scenarios. In practice, however, there is scope for debate (which can be heated by the strong views of military officers who will be expected to stake their colleagues' lives on the equipment selected) on whether 'victory' should be defined by the attainment of campaign objectives, or by a favourable

COEIA—Concept of Analysis

ratio of the opposing forces' losses in manpower and equipment, or by some other criterion. Since overall campaign results are often driven by many factors other than the particular type of equipment considered, these results may be insensitive to differences in the performance of alternative equipment options, and hence form poor discriminators for equipment selection. It may, therefore, be necessary to use some specific measures of operational effectiveness which focus on the particular type of equipment considered and which are representative of its own individual effects on the overall campaign, provided that these specific measures do not neglect any important feature of the alternative options which should influence selection for procurement, and provided that their synthesis into a single measure for presentation of the COEIA results does not introduce prejudice or bias. Given modern media exposure of military operations and public sensitivity to losses sustained and inflicted, it may also be necessary to take into account, as well as the traditional measures of military effectiveness, the likely extent of casualties to UK or allied forces and to the civilians (friendly and hostile) in the combat areas of the scenario(s) modelled, and to procure equipment which keeps those casualties at a politically-acceptable level.

Period of analysis

The time period covered by any particular COEIA study depends on the class of the equipment considered, on the availability/longevity of the alternative options, on the timing of the funding available, and on other factors. In general the COEIA should begin at the point at which the relevant procurement decision becomes effective by the assignment of funding, and should end some 25 years later to correspond approximately with the anticipated life span of major items of defence equipment. If a longer timescale is chosen, it extends into the period when it becomes impossibly difficult to forecast the military situations within which the chosen equipment would operate and hence difficult to assess the effect of alternative procurement decisions. If a shorter timescale is chosen, the study gives undue emphasis to expenditure on procurement and on support in the early years of the equipment's service life, while omitting support expenditure in later years; furthermore, the results of the study may be dominated by assumptions on the residual value of the equipment.

Interactions

The concept of analysis should identify any significant interaction between the equipment project addressed by the COEIA and other concurrent projects whose success or otherwise might affect the result of the COEIA or the EAC decision to which the COEIA contributes. It should also note any possible delays to the COEIA which might arise from the late delivery of data from supporting trials or analyses.

Management

The COEIA study and the resulting Dossier paper for a major project are the joint responsibility of the relevant one-star Defence Staff Officer and the Procurement Executive project officer. This 'dual-key' arrangement reflects these officers' respective responsibilities to their seniors on the Equipment Approvals Committee (the Vice Chief of Defence Staff and the Chief of Defence Procurement), and ensures the maintenance of a consensus on the conduct of the COEIA and its recommendations. These officers are the leading members of a steering group which should include representatives of the Service operational and support branches involved, of the Centre for Defence Analysis, of specialist branches of PE, and others as appropriate. The Chairmanship of this steering group is often held by the Defence Staff Officer, but in some circumstances it is convenient for the PE project officer to take the leading role. The two officers responsible for the COEIA appoint more-junior members of their staffs to direct detailed studies of the operational effectiveness and the life cycle cost of the alternative equipment options. It is important that the studies of operational effectiveness and of cost remain consistent with each other and with the original concept of analysis, so the two leading officers responsible for the COEIA must ensure that the operational effectiveness and costs studies do not introduce individualistic and unapproved assumptions, and that both respond harmoniously to any exogenous changes to the programme. But apart from this supervision

COEIA—Concept of Analysis

(which must be sufficient to preclude misunderstandings and divergence), the studies of operational effectiveness and of cost may be conducted almost independently, which helps to restrict access to classified military information and to commercial-in-confidence proposals from potential contractors.

The operational effectiveness and cost forecasting studies are often undertaken by the Centre for Defence Analysis in DERA and by the Directorate of Cost Forecasting in MoD (PE), respectively, but they may also be done by groups in the MoD Central Staffs, in the Defence Research Agency and in industry as the COEIA management considers most effective and efficient. However the studies are done, the Directorate of Cost Forecasting has a wide professional responsibility to ensure that all cost forecasts for the MoD are produced to the highest practicable standards, and the Deputy Chief Scientist (Scrutiny & Analysis) has the overall responsibility, advised by other branches, for scrutiny of the methodology and input data used in the COEIA before its results are presented to the EAC.

CHAPTER 4
INVESTMENT APPRAISAL

Investment Appraisal (IA) provides a structured method of assessing all the costs, benefits and risks associated with alternative decisions on public expenditure. This method is used by various UK government organisations for:

>a.) commercial appraisal of trading activities where the benefits are measured by the financial receipts from sales or charges;
>b.) cost/benefit analyses which attempt to quantify in financial terms costs and benefits which are not marketed (or for which the market price does not reflect the true economic costs); and
>c.) cost/effectiveness analyses which compare the alternative costs of achieving a specified level of effectiveness which is not assigned a monetary value.

Most IA undertaken in the MoD are in the third category (cost/effectiveness analysis), and seek to identify from alternatives the option which most economically achieves a specified objective of defence policy, which may be a high-level objective relating to the capability of UK Services or a lower-level objective relating to the output of a particular military unit or branch. Accordingly MoD IA can be used to assess alternative logistic or asset management policies, as well as options in equipment procurement, but since this paper is concerned with COEIA's role in equipment procurement only that last application of IA is considered below. The principles and procedures of investment appraisal by UK government departments are fully described in a Technical Guide[1] produced by the Treasury.

The key factors of the IA part of a COEIA are:

>a.) rigorous and comprehensive description in a Master Data and Assumptions List (MDAL) of each of the options considered, noting all the data and assumptions (on technical, procurement,

Investment Appraisal

operational, support and financial features) relevant to the option's life cycle cost;
b.) forecasts of all the components of the life cycle cost of each of the alternative options; the life cycle cost of a defence equipment project (also known variously as 'whole life cost' and as 'through life cost') includes all the expenditure directly and indirectly associated with the project from its inception to its disposal, as shown in Annex A; the costs in future years should be discounted using the current Treasury discount rate;
c.) consideration of the uncertainties in the forecast cost, performance and other characteristics of the alternative options, and of the effect of these uncertainties on the IA results;
d.) discussion of those advantages and disadvantages of different options which cannot be expressed in terms of money.

Master Data and Assumptions List

The MDAL defining the alternative equipment options (using a mixture of data and assumptions in accordance with the amount of information available on each option) must be approved by all relevant MoD branches before definitive cost forecasting begins. The MDAL includes:

a.) a complete technical description of each of the options (noting in particular any non-standard features);
b.) a definition of the procurement strategy and the development and production plans of the various contractors involved;
c.) the delivery schedule and the associated establishment of operational units, policies for these units' deployment, training and logistics, and plans for procurement of the associated infrastructure and support equipment;
d.) assumptions on the intensity of peacetime operations and on the equipment's Reliability and Maintainability (R&M), and consequent estimates of the levels of Service and/or civilian manpower required for operations, support, etc.

The generation of a MDAL demands a rigorous review of all key data and assumptions relevant to each option's costs, and accordingly ensures that all key issues have been addressed, that each option forms a self-consistent entity, and that all options are on a level playing field without inequitable benefits or penalties. The MDAL also provides a reference point from which the effect on an option's cost of any later changes in the planned characteristics of the equipment and/or in the associated procurement or support programmes can be assessed. The fundamental importance of the MDAL is reflected in the extensive discussions which are often required before it is accepted by all the Service and civilian branches involved.

Cost forecasting

Forecasts of the components of life cycle cost are derived for a COEIA using a variety of methods appropriate to the level of information on the equipment project considered.[2] At the earliest stages of the project's life cycle (when very little information is available), parametric methods may be used to derive approximate cost forecasts from the target performance parameters of the future equipment, using analytical relationships[3] between the costs and performance parameters of past projects in the same class. Later, when the leading design characteristics of the future equipment have been established by initial-design studies, parametric methods derive cost forecasts for the new equipment using both its performance parameters and its design characteristics. When the future equipment has been more fully defined, more-detailed parametric methods can be used to forecast costs at the subsystem level and to combine these costs, making due allowance for assembly and integration, to obtain more-accurate cost forecasts; this process is called synthetic forecasting. Much later, when work packages covering the various processes and activities involved in development, production, operation and support of the new equipment have been individually specified, a definitive cost forecast can be based on the volume and unit cost of the resources (man-hours, materials, fuel, etc.) required by each work package.

Cost forecasts for each equipment option in a COEIA are normally produced for MoD by the Directorate of Cost Forecasting[4] using its database on the costs of past projects, its array of costing methodologies

Investment Appraisal

relevant to the different components of life cycle cost, and any inputs from potential contractors and from the relevant Service operating and support branches. The Project Director may modify these cost forecasts, using his own specialist knowledge of a particular equipment or contractor, and remains responsible and accountable for the cost forecasts presented to the EAC in the Project Costing Certificate.

Financial assumptions

It is normal in the MoD to express future expenditure in real terms, at a given set of price levels corresponding to a particular date (generally at the middle of the current or preceding Financial Year). This policy was adopted because cost analyses of past projects are often based on real resources (such as numbers of man-hours and quantities of materials or energy) rather than on inflation-prone financial data, and consequently cost forecasts for future projects are generated initially in terms of resources and subsequently transformed into financial terms using a specified set of prices. The adjustment at a later stage of such expenditure forecasts to a different price level should, where possible, take account of the actual price changes for the labour, materials and services involved in the procurement and in-service cost of the equipment, rather than using a general retail price index which may be misleading. It is also mandatory to exclude 'sunk' costs which have already been incurred or irrevocably committed, since these costs cannot be affected by the result of the COEIA, but all future discretionary costs associated with each equipment option should be included.

Since all options in a COEIA normally refer to the same type of equipment (e.g. attack helicopters), it is unnecessary to include costs which would be common for all the alternative options. For example, if it were planned that in peacetime all the alternative attack helicopters would operate from the same bases and would use the same maintenance base for major servicing, then the fixed costs of these bases need not be included in the IA; however, any additional operating and support costs associated in future years with one of the options (including the cost of all additional land and infrastructure which it might require, and conversely the revenue from any sales which become possible because that option's requirements differ from those of its rivals and/or from equipment now in service) should be included in the IA. In force-mix studies, however, the diverse classes of equipment considered have few if any common cost components, and these studies should use the full life cycle cost including all relevant support systems and infrastructure.

In principle, investment appraisal may consider expenditure either at market prices or at factor cost (i.e. excluding indirect taxes and subsidies). The Treasury's Technical Guide directs that options attracting different Value Added Tax (VAT) conventions should be assessed on a consistent basis. Since VAT conventions on military equipment vary with the nature and origin of the equipment options considered, MoD IA normally exclude VAT. It is important, however, that budgetary cost estimates, which are made to ensure that the costs of a particular project fall within the MoD funding available, include both VAT and any common costs (see preceding paragraph) omitted from an IA. The Guide also stipulates that macroeconomic benefits to the Treasury from employment effects, generating more taxes and lower public expenditure on social benefits, should not be generally included since such macroeconomic effects arise from the overall level of government expenditure rather than from a particular equipment project. But, although such macroeconomic effects are omitted from the COEIA, the different impact of alternative procurement options on UK's level of employment and balance of trade would be discussed in the Dossier paper dealing with Procurement Strategy and would be considered by the EAC (and, for major projects, by the Cabinet) in its selection of the best equipment option. Similarly the security and commercial benefits to the UK of maintaining an indigenous capability in particular defence technologies or an indigenous defence industrial base may be considered by the EAC or at higher level.

Residual value

For a COEIA covering an agreed period, it is implicitly assumed that the military capability is required up to the end of the period, after which the equipment goes for disposal. This notional convention is adopted to

Investment Appraisal

balance the comparison in favour of those options which could if required sustain a military capability afterwards, and against those options which have negligible capability at the end of the agreed period. It is therefore necessary to estimate the revenue from sales or the costs of disposal of the equipment at the end of the period; this revenue or cost constitutes the residual value which should be identified clearly in the discussion of the IA results. Fortunately it is unnecessary for these estimates to be very accurate, since the discount factor ensures that revenues or costs at the end of the COEIA period are much less important than similar revenues or costs at the beginning of the period.

Discounting

The forecast expenditures and receipts associated with each of the alternative equipment options in an IA are distributed through the time period chosen for the study (an illustrative distribution is shown in Fig 2b), and different options often have very different time profiles of net expenditure. Net expenditure in different years cannot be compared directly because individuals and organisations recognise the time value of money and prefer to receive cash sooner rather than later and to pay bills later rather than sooner; this time value exists even if inflation is zero. Expenditure in different years of the IA period may be put on the same basis by applying a discount factor $1/(1+r)^n$ to future expenditure, where r is the real discount rate (which for an individual might be the real interest rate of money lent or borrowed) and n is the number of years until the future expenditure will be incurred. The Net Present Value (NPV) of a particular project is the sum of the discounted values of the annual net expenditures £$_n$ in future years,[5] and represents the capital sum which could now be allocated to meet all future expenditure on a particular project. It follows that two projects which have the same NPV would impose the same burden on UK Government funding, even when the expenditure profiles of the two projects are very different.

The discount rate specified by HM Treasury serves as the cost of capital and ensures that the use of resources by central government is no less efficient at the margin than in the private sector. The current discount rate

$r = 6$ per cent is set equal to the pre-tax cost of long-term capital for low risk projects in the private sector; this discount rate diminishes the importance of expenditure in future years, as illustrated in the table below.

Year	0	10	20	30
Expenditure in year, £	1	1	1	1
Discounted value of expenditure, £	1	0.56	0.31	0.17

Risk and uncertainty

At the start of a procurement programme to meet a given Staff Requirement, the MoD cannot be sure that the final performance of the equipment, and the timescale and cost of its procurement, will be as predicted. These uncertainties will not be resolved until service trials are complete and the procurement bills are paid; uncertainties about operating and support cost persist through the equipment's service life. Uncertainties about equipment which can be bought off-the-shelf from a reliable contractor, offering fixed prices and long-term guarantees, are a great deal smaller than those associated with underdeveloped projects with glossy brochures from inexperienced contractors in a country undergoing revolution.

The uncertainties about any project arise from adverse events or delays which may affect the programme, and from variations from the forecast values of the equipment's performance, reliability, cost and other characteristics. The likelihood and impact of these adverse events, and the scale of variation of the equipment's final characteristics, either may be quantified with confidence from relevant evidence on similar equipment, or may be assigned quantitative values based on judgement or inspiration, or may be virtually unquantifiable (such as the policy changes which might arise from a future election in an allied nation involved in a collaborative project).

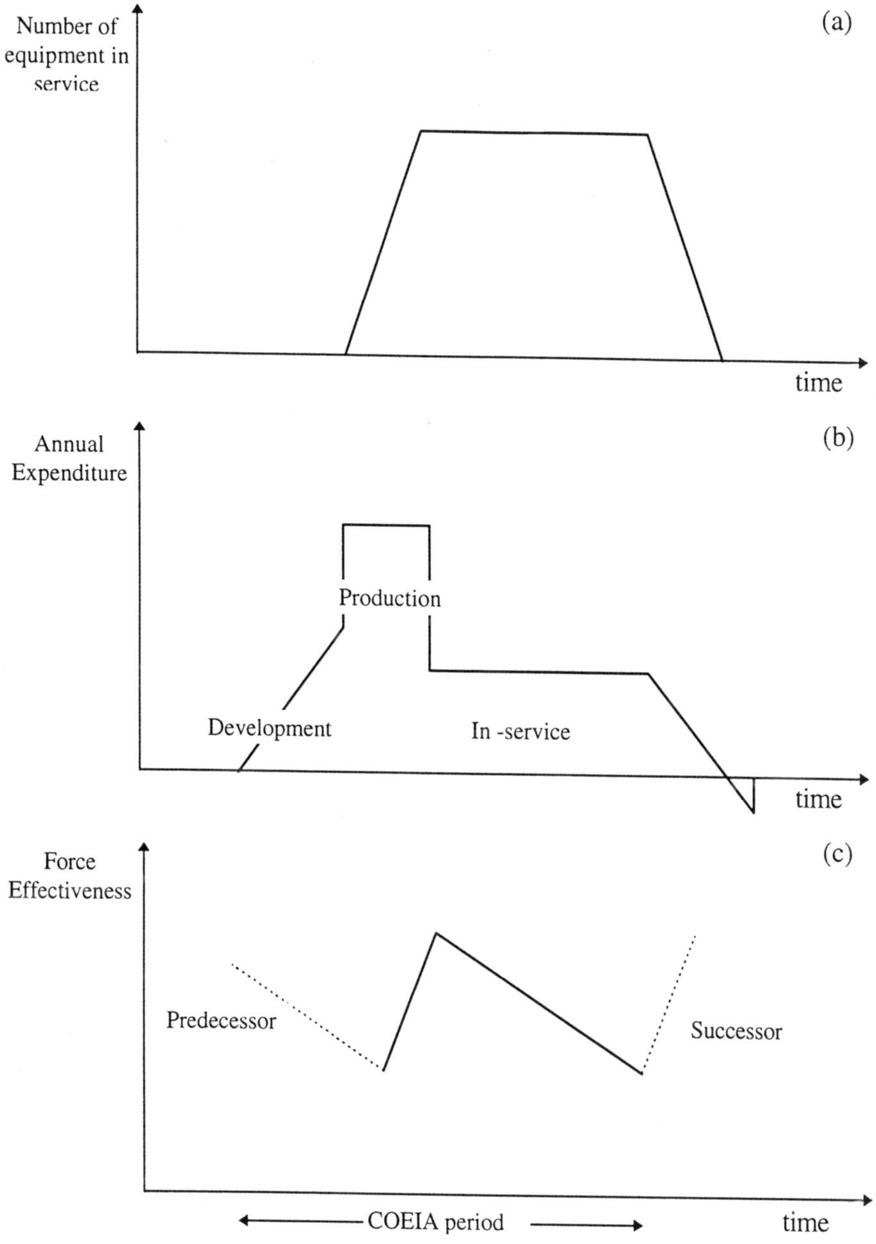

Investment Appraisal

Fig 2. Variations with time of number, expenditure and effectiveness.

Some financial literature draws the distinction between 'risks', where the probabilities of different outcomes can be estimated precisely, and 'uncertainties' where they cannot. In defence procurement, however, there are few uncertainties which can be quantified with actuarial precision, so this distinction is not very helpful. Current MoD guidelines for project management stipulate that the likelihood and impact of each uncertainty (and their product which is called 'risk') should be assessed and should be discussed, together with appropriate risk management plans, in the Procurement Issues and Strategy paper which forms part of the EAC Dossier. Such risks result from technical, industrial, financial or political problems affecting the project, and the associated risk management plans can range from early prototyping of key components to buying foreign currency forward. Risk management plans generally increase the expected cost of a project, but reduce the likelihood and/or the scale of potential variations in cost.

Current MoD procedures stipulate that the forecast costs of equipment projects should take explicit account of risk and uncertainty by expressing the forecast as three values—the Expected Cost and the Upper and Lower Costs. The Upper and Lower Costs are calculated such that there is 95 per cent confidence that the actual cost of the project will fall between them. At the early stages of many projects this procedure produces a very wide range, but at later stages when major funding decisions are required the gap between Upper and Lower Costs must have been reduced to an acceptable level using the results of studies and experiments during feasibility studies and project definition.

Affordability

The procedures of IA take no explicit account of peaks and troughs in an option's expenditure profile, all of which are compounded within the NPV total. But in practice the MoD, and any other Government Department, must keep its overall annual expenditures within the limits set by the Government's plans for taxation, borrowing and expenditure; it may therefore be impractical to select a project which demands a sharp spike in expenditure. But an option with an attractive NPV should not be

Investment Appraisal

excluded from consideration because its annual expenditure has large fluctuations, since the MoD's budget might possibly be reallocated to accommodate the fluctuations or negotiations with the relevant contractor might yield a much more acceptable profile for a small increase in overall cost.

Notes

1. HM Treasury, *Economic Appraisal in Central Government—a Technical Guide for Government Departments*, (HMSO, London, 1991).
2. D. W. Daniel, *Life Cycle Costing: Concepts, Problems, Structures and Databases* SAE Technical Paper 861786 Proc. Aerospace Technology Conference, October 1986.
3. S. A. Merridew, *The New Approach to Parametric Cost Estimating*, Proc. of 11th Annual Conference of SCAF, 20 September 1994.
4. E Lomas, *The New Cost Forecasting Organisation in MoD*, Proc. of RAeS Conference, 25 October 1995.
5. In mathematical terms $NPV = \Sigma_0^N £_n / (1 +r)^n$

CHAPTER 5
OPERATIONAL EFFECTIVENESS

There are several ways in which the performance and other characteristics of defence equipment may be assessed, and by which the relative merit of alternative equipment options may be compared. Formerly such assessments were often done by comparison with a range of minimum criteria specified in the Staff Requirement, or by a system of scoring the equipment's various attributes and combining the scores using weighting factors to derive a figure of merit. Within a COEIA, it is mandatory that the assessment should use operational analysis. The two former methods have the advantage that they can be based on the assessment of the most-likely *performance* of the new equipment (which can be well defined if the equipment is already in service elsewhere but would be more speculative if it is at the early stages of development), but the operational analysis method requires assessment of the new equipment's *effectiveness* against other equipment which is in service with or on order for the armed forces of potentially-hostile nations, and which may have its critical design and performance characteristics shrouded in secrecy.

Former assessment methods

The simplest former approach to equipment assessment was to list all the attributes of the class of equipment considered which contribute to its operational effectiveness—for an AFV these attributes would include the range and lethality of its gun, the protection offered by its armour, the speed and terrain-crossing capability provided by its engine and tracks, etc.—and to set minimum acceptable levels for each attribute. The next step was to compare the design and performance characteristics of each option with the list of specified minima, and to exclude those options which failed to achieve the minimum standards in one or more criteria. The remaining options, which meet all the criteria, could then be regarded as operationally equivalent, and the cheapest could be selected for procurement. This approach had the virtue of giving potential contractors

Operational Effectiveness

clear design and performance targets towards which to direct their proposals, and of making the selection process very straightforward (provided MoD staff could overcome the difficulties of providing independent estimates of cost and performance to validate contractors' proposals). However, this approach had the disadvantage that even relatively-simple military systems have as many as 50 relevant performance and design criteria, and complex systems can have an order of magnitude more. Unless the minimum criteria were set very low, some options which were generally acceptable could be excluded by falling short of a very few criteria. Furthermore, options received no credit for outperforming the minimum criteria, even in attributes where this should yield some military advantage.

Another former approach was to set up a scoring and weighting system so that an option's strengths and weaknesses in different performance characteristics could be synthesised into a single overall score. In some cases a small number of key performance criteria were designated as mandatory, thereby rejecting equipment options which failed to satisfy these key criteria and avoiding the danger of implying that shortfalls in any of these areas could be offset by good performance in other areas. For example, satisfactory values for aircraft landing distance, ship stability and AFV armour protection are absolutely necessary for the overall effectiveness of these equipments. The scoring and weighting approach claimed the virtue of consistency across the alternative equipment options, but actually introduced into the assessment a high level of subjectivity (although there was scope via sensitivity analysis to test the robustness of the result to the chosen values of scoring and weighting factors). This method needed a scoring system for each of the very many aspects of performance to translate an equipment option's actual performance into a rating between ideal and unacceptable, a weighting system to reflect the different importance of different aspects of performance, and a method of combining the weighted scores (scalar addition is only one possibility among many).

Both these former methods had the disadvantage of comparing one unit of equipment against another, rather than comparing the effectiveness of

33

the alternative forces of these units or possibly of some mix of the alternative equipments, which could be procured, operated and supported for the same expenditure (expressed as NPV). These methods therefore cannot address the possible advantages and disadvantages of deploying many low-costs systems rather than a few expensive ones. The selection process is thus significantly constrained and is unlikely to yield best value for money.

Another disadvantage of these former methods was reliance on what their supporters could call expert professional judgement and what their critics could call arbitrary and subjective opinion. In practice, the implementation of the two former methods lay between these two extremes, depending on the professionalism of the officers and officials concerned. In any list of requirements for a new equipment compiled by military staff, some requirements arose inevitably and logically from the nature of the equipments' environment and from the laws of physics which govern the equipments' operation. But many more requirements represented the Defence Staff's collective judgement of desirable performance and design characteristics for the next generation of equipment. These judgements, however expert and honest, were inevitably subjective and did not facilitate debate on the trade off between one individual requirement and another, or between a requirement and the equipment's cost. Similarly in a scoring and weighting system there was no objective method of determining the relationship (linear, non-linear?) between a performance or design characteristic of the equipment considered and its allocated score. Nor was there an objective method of assigning weighting factors to a large number (perhaps hundreds) of design and performance characteristics. While a complete scoring and weighting system based on a consensus of expert assessment did demonstrate implicit judgements of the trade offs between equipment characteristics, it did not address the trade off between performance and cost (unless cost was incorporated in the scoring system) and it could not convincingly demonstrate impartiality between alternative equipment options.

Operational analysis

The method favoured for COEIA employs military operational analysis

Operational Effectiveness

(OA) at a lower and more-detailed level than in force-mix studies, to evaluate explicitly and quantitatively the overall *effectiveness* of the equipment option considered, where *effectiveness* depends on the option's success relative to an enemy's current equipment while an equipment option's *performance* is an absolute and enduring set of characteristics. Experience in the operational analysis of military operations has been progressively built up since its genesis during the Second World War, with studies of anti-submarine warfare and of radar-based air defence. OA studies cannot predict the results of individual battles, which are often determined by luck or inspiration, but it can identify trends linking the probability of victory to the number and effectiveness of the weapons systems deployed by the opposing forces. Such trends enable OA studies to conclude that one equipment option is likely to do better than another, and this conclusion forms an input to the COEIA.

Currently OA studies to support COEIA use a range of combat models developed at the Centre for Defence Analysis and elsewhere. Depending on the nature of the scenario(s) and of the equipment itself, an option could be assessed when operating singly, or as part of a homogeneous group, or as part of a heterogeneous force mix. In some cases this OA may yield a single measure of equipment effectiveness, but generally the outcome of military operations must be assessed in terms of a small set of effectiveness measures for each scenario and operation considered. The number of effectiveness measures generally varies according to the level of operation considered; in low-level studies there may be up to half a dozen effectiveness measures (such as merchant ships sunk, escorts and hostile submarines destroyed in a convoy battle), but in high-level studies the number of measures tends to decrease, ultimately to a single criterion of victory or defeat in war. Thus the OA approach does not entirely remove the problem of assessing equipment options in terms of multiple parameters, but it does greatly simplify the problem by drastically reducing the number of different parameters to be assessed.

As well as the results of combat models in various scenarios, the assessment may have to consider additional equipment characteristics (such as logistics and strategic mobility) which may not be fully reflected

Choose Your Weapon

in COEIA-level OA. However, even when these characteristics are added to the results of combat modelling, the number of parameters which must be synthesised to obtain the overall effectiveness of an equipment option are generally one or two orders of magnitude fewer than the number of performance parameters which were formerly assessed by scoring and weighting methods.

One critical advantage of OA is that, while disagreements about performance criteria or about scoring and weighting systems are virtually impossible to resolve, the individual uncertainties about aspects of an OA can each be debated constructively. In many cases such uncertainties can be resolved by further intelligence information or data from exercises and trials, and in other cases the range of uncertainty can be bounded by the limits of technical and military credibility. In all OA studies, the input data and assumptions should be explicitly presented, and justified (as far as possible) by reference to supporting factual evidence.

Variation of effectiveness with time

The effectiveness of any particular combat equipment option tends to vary through the COEIA period as the relevant enemy equipment is upgraded by applying the latest technology to enhance individual aspects of its performance, or is replaced by more-advanced equipment with significantly greater overall effectiveness. For this reason, and also because of that option's particular delivery schedule, the effectiveness of UK Forces resulting from procurement of that option will vary through the COEIA period (as illustrated in Fig 2c). Each of the alternative procurement options will exhibit its own characteristic variation of force effectiveness, and these variations may differ significantly when some options involve delayed procurement of new equipment. There are several alternative ways of assessing the time profiles of force effectiveness; if the timing of a conflict were predictable, the options could be compared in terms of their effectiveness in that year; if a malevolent enemy was awaiting a favourable moment to strike, any substantial (albeit temporary) drop in effectiveness would be unacceptable and options could be compared in terms of their minimum effectiveness; if a conflict were equally likely at any point through the COEIA period, the alternative options could be compared in terms of their average effectiveness over time.

Uncertainty of OA

Although OA provides the preferred method of assessing the effectiveness of an equipment option, it is inevitable that its results are subject to a greater degree of uncertainty than is associated with the results of methods based on that option's predicted performance. In OA studies, uncertainties about an equipment option's performance are compounded by uncertainties about the performance of enemy and allied equipment, about the terrain and weather conditions of a future battlefield, and about the validity of analytical combat modelling. Such uncertainties were always present, but they were often tacitly disregarded by the former assessment methods. The problem of uncertainty is magnified because (thanks to successful deterrence) UK Armed Forces are only rarely engaged in major conflicts which enable the effectiveness of their current military equipment to be observed, quantified and used to validate OA models of the relevant class of equipment. Formerly some OA studies have taken little account of uncertainty, or have included only a cursory sensitivity analysis using arbitrary variations (such as 10 per cent) of some input parameters whose effects were often consigned to an annex of the study report. Although there is currently no formal requirement for three-point estimates of effectiveness to correspond to three-point cost forecasts (discussed in Chapter 4), the EAC Guidelines stipulate that the OA study supporting a COEIA should have an explicit and well-considered strategy for dealing with uncertainty and demonstrating its impact on the study's results. Visibility of the uncertainties, as well as of the expected values of the effectiveness of alternative equipment options, is required to help EAC select a robust option, whose cost effectiveness is superior in most credible situations.

CHAPTER 6
SYNTHESIS AND PRESENTATION OF RESULTS

At the end of the COEIA study, the assessments of operational effectiveness and forecasts of life cycle costs of the alternative equipment options must be brought together in a comparison to determine which option offers best value for money. This may be done by plotting on a graph the forecast values of force effectiveness and life cycle cost (expressed as NPV) of each alternative option (as shown in Fig 3). This procedure correctly reflects the two-dimensional character of cost-effectiveness as a concept, but it is not entirely satisfactory because while Option 3 is clearly better than 2 or 4, it is not obvious whether it is better than 1 or 5. Ideally the the options should be formulated to reveal which force offers the lowest NPV of life cycle cost at a given level of military effectiveness, or which offers the greatest level of military effectiveness at a chosen NPV (see Fig 4).

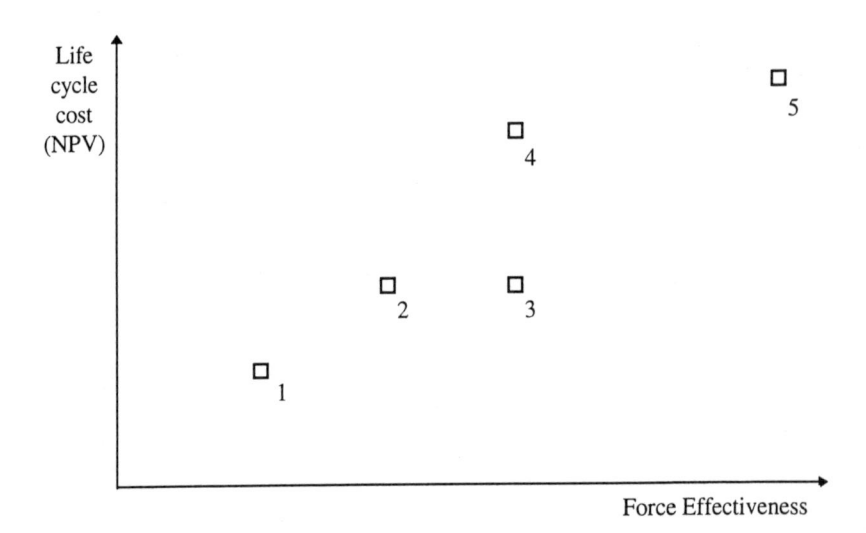

Fig 3. Comparison of cost and effectiveness of five alternative options.

Synthesis and Presentation of Results

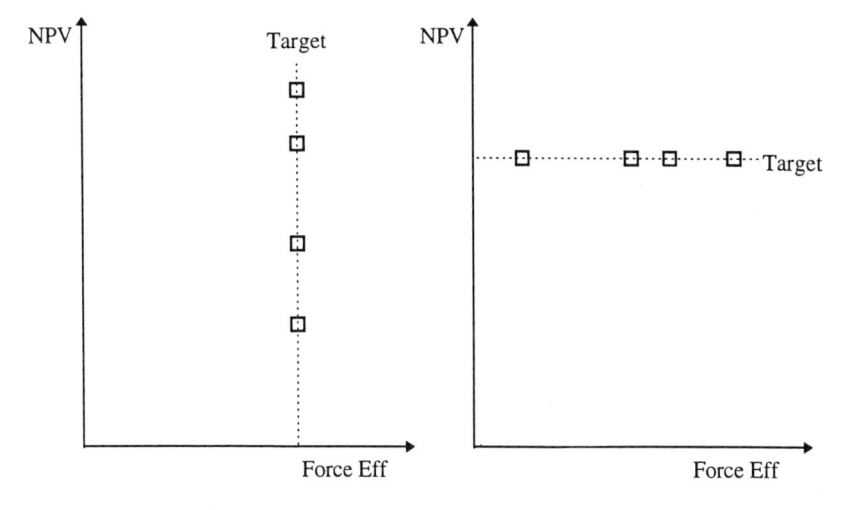

Fig 4. Comparison at constant effectiveness or constant cost

The former option is in accordance with normal public sector management, seeking the most economical method of achieving a policy goal. However, in COEIA the complexities inherent in military OA generally make it impractical to tailor the number and quality of weapons systems deployed to achieve a particular level of military force effectiveness (without an exorbitant number of expensive simulated campaigns), and it is generally easier in practice to tailor the alternative forces to attain a specified level of NPV. There are some dangers also in this policy, since negotiations with a contractor in parallel to a COEIA may produce fresh cost information which invalidates the earlier forecasts of the one or more components of the life cycle cost of one of the alternative equipment options. Fortunately such fresh information, while it may be very significant in one part of the project, does not in general affect the overall NPV sufficiently to justify derivation of different force levels having the original specified NPV and recalculation of these forces' military effectiveness; a comparison of alternative options with NPV values which are

Choose Your Weapon

similar, but not identical, is often adequate to identify the option offering best value for money. In accordance with this policy the scale of procurement of new equipment is varied for each equipment option to determine the force effectiveness associated with a particular level of life cycle cost.

When the variation of the life cycle cost of a military force with the number of equipments deployed is a (virtually) continuous function, it is relatively straightforward to derive force levels which are based on different equipment options but which have the same (or similar) levels of the NPV of expenditure. But in other cases, the variation is not continuous, because equipment must be procured in whole numbers (e.g. 9 or 10 warships, not 9.5) and because military organisation and military bases are not infinitely flexible. In such cases (as illustrated in Fig 5) the life cycle cost of a force will jump as additional units of equipment are procured, as additional squadrons or battalions are formed, and as additional bases are activated.

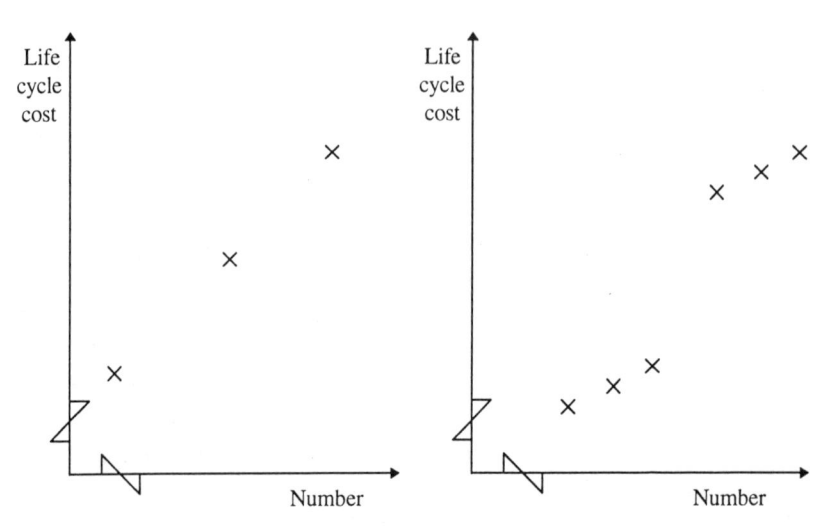

Fig 5. Variation of Force Cost with Number of Units in service.

Synthesis and Presentation of Results

Similarly options involving enhancements to existing equipment are constrained by the limited numbers of such equipment available, and in such cases the force cannot be expanded to attain specified levels of force effectiveness or of NPV. Even if additional equipments were available, the number of units deployed may be bounded by the constraints of military manpower which cannot be sharply increased (or decreased) to accommodate the requirements of an equipment option. In theory there are inumerable possible permutations of performance, reliability and cost, but in practice it is unreasonable to burden a soldier in the field with two radios with high failure rates rather than one reliable system.

It is therefore not generally possible to reduce the cost and effectiveness of all the diverse alternative options from a two-dimensional problem to a one-dimensional ranking of options. The new equipment options may generally be scaled to match a target of life cycle cost (as shown in Fig 6) using MoD forecasts of the cost and effectiveness of increasing numbers of equipments and/or contractor's proposals of the costs of various batch sizes. The scaled values can then be compared on that Figure with the 'do-nothing' option and with various upgrades of existing equipment. The COEIA procedure illuminates the relative merits of the alternative equipment options, and in some cases may be able to rank them definitively, but the identification of the best option (even in military and financial terms only) demands expert judgement from the EAC and its advisers.

The presentation of COEIA results must reflect the uncertainties (which may differ between one option and another, and may in some cases be very considerable) in the assessments of operational effectiveness and the forecasts of life cycle cost. The effect of some risks (on, for example, the final achieved performance or cost of defence equipment under development) may be represented by upper and lower confidence limits on the forecasts of the equipment's operational effectiveness and on the NPV of its life cycle costs (as discussed in Chapters 4 and 5). These confidence limits may in turn be represented by expanding the point representing that equipment on a cost-effectiveness graph into an area of uncertainty, which is shown (see Fig 7) as circular but may in practice be asymetrical,

Choose Your Weapon

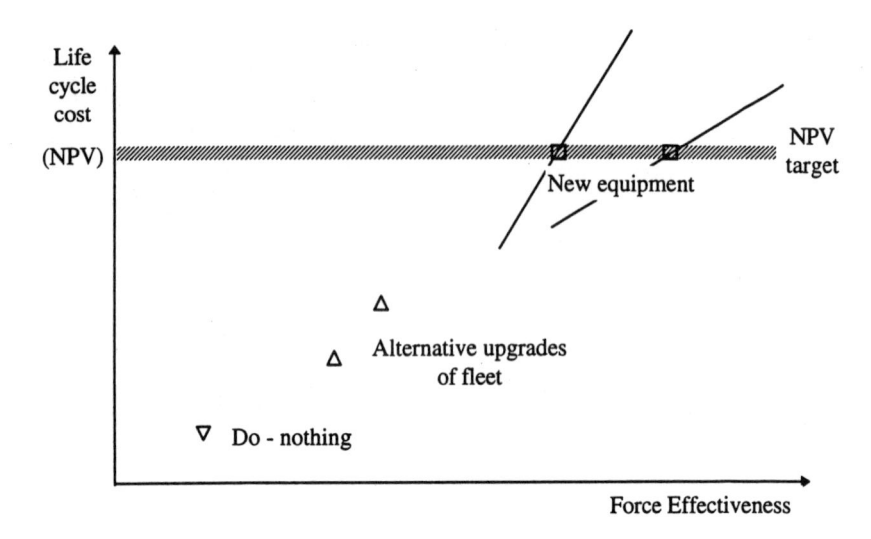

Fig 6. Two dimensional comparison of the cost and effectiveness of alternative options.

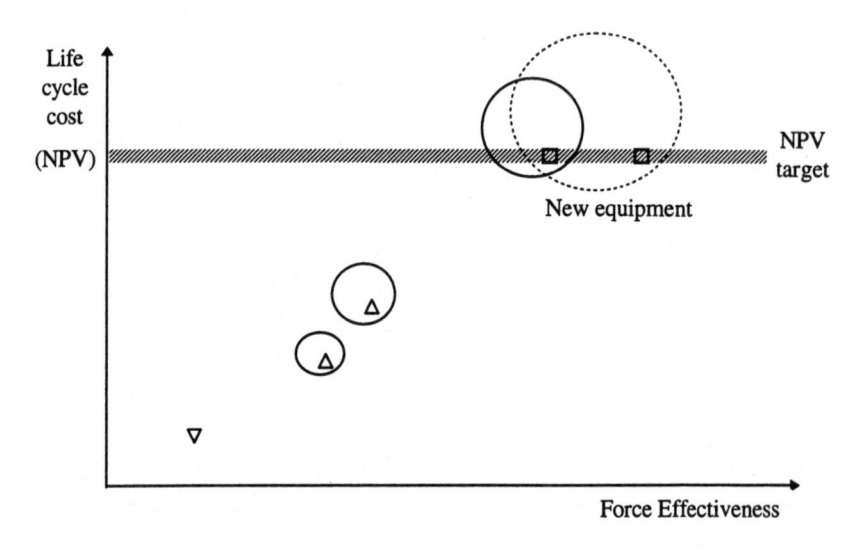

Fig 7. Areas of uncertainty around forecast cost and effectiveness of alternative options.

Synthesis and Presentation of Results

which may be offset towards lower performance and higher cost to allow for the greater likelihood (in view of the extensive experience enshrined in Murphy's Law) of shortfalls in performance and overruns on cost, and which is larger for new projects relying on advanced technology. The comparative assessment of the alternative equipment options would then be influenced not only by the position of the points representing the expected cost and effectiveness of the options, but by the size and shape of the areas of uncertainty around them.

The effect of the other uncertainties, whose likelihood cannot be realistically estimated, can best be demonstrated by sensitivity analysis, calculating 'what if' a nation collaborating on the project were to change its priorities or 'what if' a new material, despite exhaustive trials, proved less robust in actual service than expected. The results of these 'what if' calculations on any of the alternative options may be plotted as arrows from the point representing its cost and effectiveness (see Fig 8), but it remains a matter of political, military or technical judgement (depending on the nature of the uncertainty) on which of them need be taken more seriously than the others during project selection.

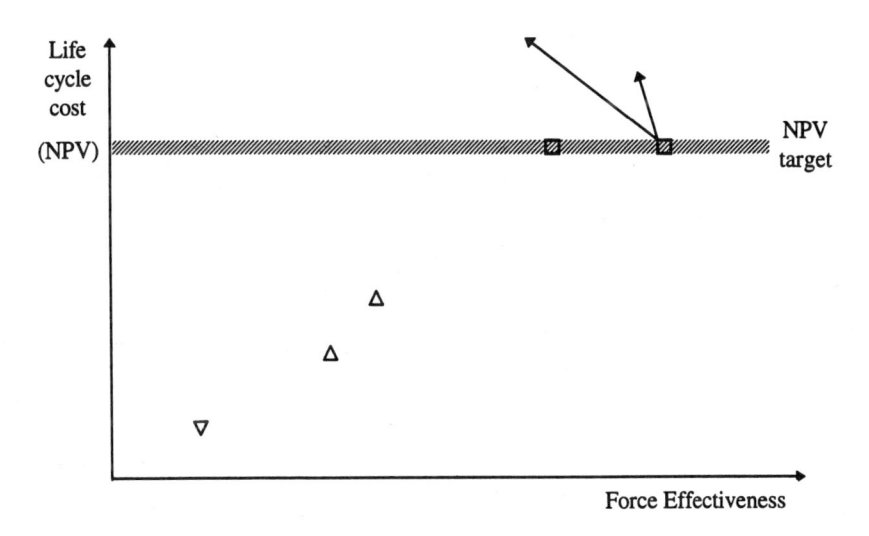

Fig 8. Effects of exogenous uncertainty on one option.

Choose Your Weapon

The COEIA may conclude, after consideration of the confidence limits on forecasts of effectiveness and cost, that one of the alternative options is very likely to provide the most attractive combination of effectiveness and cost. That conclusion does not, however, imply that the associated equipment is free from risks and uncertainties, but merely that these risks and uncertainties are not large enough to erode that option's lead over the next-best alternative. When the COEIA has identified the most cost-effective option in military and financial terms, the EAC Dossier must combine that conclusion with other papers' inputs on industrial, financial, foreign policy and other relevant issues, and present to the EAC a recommendation for the procurement of the equipment option (or mix of options) which provide best overall value for money, taking account of all the MoD's objectives.

CHAPTER 7
APPLICATIONS

Since its adoption by the MoD a few years ago, the COEIA procedure has been used to support the procurement of a variety of defence equipment. These applications have re-emphasised the enduring principle that it is more difficult to assess the military effectiveness of a multi-function, multi-attribute defence equipment which interacts in its operation with many other classes of equipment, than to assess a single-role equipment operating in isolation (just as families find it more difficult to choose a motor car to meet their various physical and psychological requirements than to select a spanner to service it). They have also re-emphasised that it is often more difficult to assess quantitatively the contributions of equipment providing essential but indirect support (communications, logistics, intelligence etc.) to military operations than to assess the contributions of combat equipment which engages the enemy directly. The assessment of a communication system, for example, is complicated because of the number and nature of the subsystems (hardware and software) involved and because the system's effectiveness depends on the psychology, morale and experience of the user as well as on its own inherent performance; it follows that such systems may only be adequately assessed in terms of organisational objectives.

Multi-role systems

Where one or more of the alternative equipment options has multi-role capability, it is necessary to compare the operational effectiveness and cost of a 'comparable' set of heterogeneous and homogeneous fleets, implying that the alternative fleets could perform the same set of operational roles. For example, various fleets of aircraft might be designed to be capable of air defence, close air support, interdiction and reconnaissance. In heterogeneous fleets, each aircraft type would be assigned to the role in which it was relatively most effective, but the multi-role aircraft in homogenous fleets would be switched from one role to another as the developing operational situation demanded. It follows that the flexible homogenous fleet could be less numerous, but its unit cost would be higher because each multi-role aircraft incorporates the subsystems required for each of its diverse capabilities, additional training is required to make aircrew proficient in more than one role, and a larger stock of weapons must be available to each aircraft to exploit its flexibility. For each alternative fleet, it is necessary to construct a time profile of forces showing how the equipment of the units which currently undertake those roles will be progressively replaced by one or more new equipments from the alternative options, and how the number of units deployed may change to reflect the enhanced capability of the new equipment. This time profile of forces provides in each case the basis for complementary calculations of the time profile of expenditure and of military capability. In assessing the military capability of a mixed fleet, each unit should be allocated to the task for which its equipment is better suited; thereafter the operational effectiveness of the fleet in each of its roles can be calculated, and the results aggregated over (the different roles) and different scenarios to obtain an overall measure of fleet effectiveness. While the calculation of operational effectiveness of the mixed fleet in each of its roles in each of the different scenarios is a difficult task, it is even more difficult to formulate an aggregation process which fairly reflects the different qualities of alternative equipment options. A simple arithmetical average may conceal inadequacy in a potentially-critical situation, weighting factors can introduce bias, and a product of effectiveness will condemn a fleet without capability in every single role and situation considered. The problem is compounded if the fleet might most often operate as part of a larger allied force within which roles could be reallocated. Whatever aggregation method or combination of methods is chosen, its assumptions and implications must be clearly explained. Where practicable, operational analysis of a campaign using alternative heterogeneous and homogeneous fleets should be made to determine which provides the greatest overall effectiveness, since this result is more representative than can be obtained from any aggregation process.

Assessment is even more difficult for large, complex equipment, like surface warships, which are not only capable of more than one role but

Applications

can simultaneously engage in a variety of combat activities against other warships, aircraft and submarines. It follows that warship effectiveness cannot be assessed on a one-versus-one basis (like two opposing fighter aircraft in close combat), but only as part of a maritime campaign involving the full range of relevant military units (below the sea, on its surface, in the air above, and in space beyond). In many maritime campaigns, each combat result sets the scene for the next encounter, as various different combat and supporting units are lost or degraded, whereas land and air campaigns tend to be conducted as a series of discrete operations or missions coordinated to attain a particular military objective, and as a result land and air equipment can often be assessed at mission level. However it is important not to make arbitrary distinctions between systems areas—each class of military equipment should be assessed at the appropriate level, which is a compromise between the dual needs to avoid excessive complexity in analysis and to include all significant features in the equipment's operation. In some cases, this means assessing operational effectiveness at fleet rather than at unit level.

Weapon and support systems

In defining alternative fleets (of combat aircraft, for example) it is necessary to make associated assumptions about the weapon systems to be used and about support systems (such as airborne early warning, air-to-air refuelling and logistics units) required for effective operations. For smaller and cheaper classes of equipment, like most land systems, the vehicle and its weapons and its protection are all procured together as an integrated package, and alternative options can be assessed on that basis. For air and sea equipment, however, it is not unusual for the procurement of platforms to be decoupled from at least some of their offensive and defensive weapons and support systems—aircraft can be equipped with new air-to-air and air-to-ground weapons, and ship hulls can be equipped with new weapon and sensor systems. Fortunately the alternative equipment options considered can often be associated with a common suite of assumptions about the rest of the nation's military inventory, current and planned, and in such cases the COEIA can take the inventory as given and concentrate on the alternative options. But if one of the equipment options or fleet mixes demands additional equipment or facilities, these must be included in the COEIA.

Command, Control and Communications (C^3) systems

The military effectiveness of a C^3 system controlling the many diverse units in a military force (at whatever tactical or strategic level) must be assessed in terms of the overall effectiveness of that force in agreed scenarios. The overall effectiveness may be measured either by modelling a military campaign to derive a Measure of Effectiveness for the military force in a chosen scenario, or by modelling a set of 'sample situations' within which the performance of the communication system may be evaluated and then aggregating the results in proportions representative of the chosen scenario to obtain an overall Measure of Effectiveness. The latter method has the disadvantage of introducing subjectivity in the choice of proportions, but has the compensating advantage that the results of the sample situations once calculated may be combined in any required proportions to represent alternative operations in various different scenarios. It is important, when assessing the benefits which alternative future communications, command and control systems would confer on a military force, that the deployment and operations of the force should not be constrained by the limitations of its present C^3 but should be reconsidered for each alternative future C^3 system and replanned to exploit its individual qualities and potentialities.

Costs and benefits of COEIA

The cost of the several COEIA studies at different stages of the life cycle of an equipment project varies with the scale and complexity of the project considered, but is generally below £1m. In the US a single COEA typically costs a few million dollars. The cost of COEIA studies is relatively low when they address a limited number of alternative options, whose cost and effectiveness forecasts are free from special difficulty or dispute; the cost is relatively large when the number of options is inflated to accommodate influential points of view within or beyond the MoD, when new technologies or new procurement and support strategies are

Applications

involved, or when the goalposts move in response to the changes in the geopolitical environment during the definition and development of the project. It is important to remember, however, that a substantial fraction of COEIA expenditure is not new, and would have been required under earlier procurement procedures to support budgeting, investment appraisal, and operational requirement activities.

The costs of COEIA studies have been criticised on the grounds that their recommendations generally correspond with the preconceived judgements of expert MoD officers and officials when there is clear water between the leading options, and fail to discriminate with confidence between the leading options when these options appeared in advance to offer equally-good value for money. However, when the leading options seem equally attractive, the results of COEIA help resolve the debate and support a procurement decision; when one option appears superior on military and financial grounds, a COEIA study can estimate the cost penalty which would be incurred by choosing instead one of the runners up for reasons of national industrial, financial or foreign policy. The results of COEIA studies can also help to identify key issues and set others in proper proportion. The main benefits of a *well-conducted* COEIA are that it provides a useful framework for debate on the defence equipment options considered, that it illuminates for decision makers the relative advantages and disadvantages of the alternative options, and that it provides another of the 'checks and balances' which are necessary to prevent the MoD or any other organisation from being misled into error by a tempting but unsound mirage. These benefits appear well worth the cost, which is only an infinitesimal fraction (0.5 per cent for all the COEIA studies in a project is regarded as a reasonable target) of the life cycle cost of a major defence project.

CHAPTER 8
FURTHER DEVELOPMENTS OF COEIA

'Discounting' effectiveness

Chapter 6 on the presentation of COEIA results refers, for simplicity, to one of the alternative equipment options being represented by a point (or a circle or some asymetrical area) on a graph of cost against effectiveness. However, in reality, each option is associated with a time profile of expenditure as the equipment's life cycle costs are progressively incurred as it is procured and operated in service, and with a time profile of the capability of UK Armed Forces as the equipment replaces its less-capable predecessor in service. Schematic profiles are illustrated in Fig 2. The expenditure profile is summarised by adding the discounted values of annual expenditure to obtain its Net Present Value, but there is yet no consensus on how the effectiveness profile might be summarised. In cases where the assessment of operational effectiveness of each of the alternative options demands complex and extensive analysis, it is tempting to focus the analysis on a chosen future year when all the equipment associated with each option might have entered service, and to compare the options in terms of their assessed effectiveness in that year. This approach is unsound because it neglects the differences in the military effectiveness provided in the intervening years by options with different in-service dates, and because any equipment option could enhance its apparent cost-effectiveness by delaying its procurement until just before the chosen future year in which effectiveness is assessed (thus delaying and discounting its cost, but leaving its effectiveness in the chosen year unaltered). It follows that it is necessary to take proper account of the time profile of effectiveness.

It is well recognised that in actual warfare the timely arrival of new equipment, supplies or reinforcements can tilt the balance between victory and defeat, but in peacetime the urgency of replacing obsolete equipment may be less obvious (as long as peace endures) and hard to measure against the convenience of deferring expenditure to a later year.

Further Developments of COEIA

One possible (but not yet agreed) solution would be to discount the effectiveness of an equipment option in each year of the period considered in the same way (but not necessarily by the same factor) as annual expenditures are discounted. Such discounting of effectiveness would recognise that (other things being equal) the public's time preference for security would prefer its nation to have a given level of military capability in future years 0-5 rather than in years 5-10.

This preference may be quantified (see Annex B) by discounting force effectiveness in future years using a discount factor derived from the assumed probability of a war starting in each future year of the COEIA period. This discounting procedure cannot claim to be rigorous, and in most cases, when the time profiles of military effectiveness associated with the alternative equipment options are similar, it would be unnecessary. But in cases where the time profiles are very different (for example, when some of the alternative options must enter service several years after the others), the alternative sums of discounted effectiveness may provide better representations of the alternative time profiles than either snapshots of effectiveness in a particular year, or average values across the period considered.

Costs of operations

The MoD currently measures the cost of military equipment in terms of its life cycle cost (including the total cost of procurement, operations, support and disposal) in peacetime. This policy is consistent with the historic Cold War confrontation over several decades between the forces of NATO and the Warsaw Pact, during which UK military equipment was specified and procured primarily for its capability to resist a Warsaw Pact attack on the NATO alliance, and in which the bulk of UK Forces were engaged in peaceful training in the NATO area preparing to withstand that attack. If this attack had occurred and had involved the full range of weapons deployed by the opposing forces, the consequences would have been so horrendous that the additional cost of military operations while the conflict lasted would have been only of academic interest to future archaeologists. Today however, UK Forces are routinely deployed on a variety of military tasks, in support of their assigned Defence Roles as outlined in Chapter 2. Some of those may involve protracted peacekeeping operations. The 'contingent' cost of these operations depends on their remoteness from the UK, the scale of the UK Forces involved, and the level of opposition which they confront. From a narrow MoD perspective these contingent costs may be ignored if they are sure to be met by an additional grant from the Treasury or by contributions from grateful foreigners; hence the policy of measuring equipment cost in peacetime currently remains in force.

However, it is arguable that in the twenty-first century UK Forces will be periodically deployed beyond the NATO area to engage in a range of combat, near-combat and humanitarian activities. These activities would inevitably involve more intensive and potentially-damaging operations leading to increased consumption of fuel, spares and (if and when necessary) ordnance. It is arguable that the substantial costs of deployment to an area remote from the UK, of operations and support on a hostile environment, and subsequent repatriation of the UK forces involved should be identified as part of the likely cost of any new equipment during its in-service life. If the inclusion of such costs became MoD policy, it would favour even more strongly the procurement of robust, reliable equipment, with minimal requirements for supporting personnel and engineering equipment, and providing maximum protection for the UK Servicemen deployed. Understandably there is no current consensus on the number and nature of the 'little wars' and other operations for which UK forces might be deployed abroad in the twenty-first century, but the number is most unlikely to be zero and it would be more realistic for procurement decisions to be based on calculations of life cycle cost which take account (like the assessments of effectiveness) of representative future conflict scenarios involving UK Armed Forces.

Resource Accounting

It has been decided that UK Government Departments will adopt resource accounting, as used by large commercial organisations, to provide better information for equipment management and cash planning. After

Further Developments of COEIA

this reform each Department will prepare a cash flow statement derived from the existing appropriate account, an income and expenditure account showing debtors and creditors as well as in-year payments and receipts, and a balance sheet stating the Departments' assets and liabilities. The MoD will implement resource accounting by 1 April 1998.

It is not yet clear whether the introduction of resource accounting will have any significant effect on the COEIA procedure. The provision of additional financial information will not of itself affect IA, which is and must remain based on the evaluation and discounting of annual cash flows, so it seems likely that COEIA will be virtually unaltered.

Distribution of MoD Models

Potential MoD contractors have a strong and vested interest in the COEIA procedure which is now being used to assess and compare their proposals for new defence equipment. These contractors have welcomed the presentations and discussions organised by learned societies (such as RUSI and RAeS) to illuminate the principles of COEIA, but have also sought unlimited access to the data, models and methodologies which the MoD plans to use in particular COEIA addressing specific defence equipment projects. It has now been agreed that in future, following the issue of Invitations To Tender (ITT) for a major equipment project, the MoD will brief potential contractors about the role of COEIA in the assessment process, and will also provide some information from the relevant COEIA Concept of Analysis (including the threat, the scenarios, the nature of operational effectiveness and cost models, and the principal measures of effectiveness). Such information is intended to enable potential contractors to generate proposals well suited to the MoD's requirements.

It would be unwise for the MoD to release all the information in its Concept of Analysis or to provide its own effectiveness and cost models for use by UK and foreign contractors because:

a.) the application of such models to a particular procurement problem requires familiarity with their strengths and weaknesses, and expert judgement on a range of defence operational and technology issues;

b.) costing models rely on data on past equipment projects which is confidential to MoD and to the suppliers of that equipment;

c.) it is necessary to protect classified Intelligence information about the design and performance characteristics of some equipment available to potentially-hostile nations;

d.) some scenarios and perceived threats are politically sensitive.

Even without complete exposure of MoD data, models and methodologies, expert contractors can use their own understanding of military technologies and operations to design cost-effective equipment. Each contractor can maximise his own equipment's chance of selection by providing a comprehensive response to the ITT, and by including in that response the results of sufficient technology demonstrations and risk assessment/management studies to reduce the risk and uncertainty associated with his proposal. Furthermore, as has been stated above, the COEIA result is only one of several inputs to MoD decision-making on equipment procurement.

Similar considerations preclude the publication of detailed COEIA results, though each individual contractor whose equipment is not selected is advised of MoD views on the failings of that equipment and of the information in the associated proposal. The military and financial comparison of that equipment with its rivals forms part of advice to a UK Government Minister, and is made public only at his discretion.

CHAPTER 9
THE WAY AHEAD

When the COEIA process was introduced into MoD procedures, a conscious decision was taken that MoD would issue internal Guidelines[1] to its staff rather than a prescriptive manual defining how COEIA should be done. This decision was driven by the varied characteristics of military equipment, and the recognition that some diversity of methodology (within the overall principles of COEIA) would be required to cover the whole spectrum of defence systems. This policy required that each MoD procurement branch should formulate the best method of applying COEIA principles in its own particular area (such as CIS[2]). As experience on various defence systems is accumulated, it is intended that the MoD's Internal Guidelines on COEIA should be progressively revised to incorporate the lessons learned and to provide additional guidance in problem areas.

The new Guidelines will emphasise the importance of fully defining the Concept of Analysis before the COEIA cost and effectiveness studies are begun, in order to preclude any of the branches involved moving the goalposts or tilting the playing field during the studies, and thus wasting time and effort besides provoking disputes. They will also emphasise the importance of completing the COEIA analysis in time for the results to contribute effectively to the EAC's decision making. Since the new EAC procedures and the COEIA process were introduced into an ongoing procurement programme, it was inevitable that some of the earliest studies struggled to meet programme milestones, but as experience is accumulated and the new process is integrated into procurement projects from their earliest stages, it is expected that such problems will diminish.

When the COEIA procedure was introduced, there was some concern in the Services and the defence industry that it was primarily a bureaucratic device to delay new equipment projects, and that it would disrupt the harmony of collaborative projects with allies who use different methods. But it is now increasingly accepted that a well-organised COEIA need

Choose Your Weapon

take no longer than former procedures, though the COEIA often addresses a wider range of alternatives and thus requires extra resources; furthermore, by encouraging explicit assumptions and constructive debate of key issues, the COEIA procedure may actually accelerate the quest for a satisfactory decision. While many other allied nations do not use such procedures (the United States is a notable exception and has used COEA for decades), all the major NATO nations are familiar with the concepts of military OA and participate in international discussions of the relevant techniques and methodology; on collaborative projects, therefore, there are no insuperable barriers to 'COEIA-like' studies being undertaken or directed by joint project offices to satisfy the requirements of all partner nations, even if individual nations do not have exactly identical views, for example, on the relative importance of scenarios and the scale of technical risk.

A more serious problem is the scarcity of analytical resources to undertake the COEIA studies. It is an unfortunate coincidence that the COEIA process, demanding an even-more-rigorous evaluation of a wider range of equipment options to obtain the best possible value for money from the MoD's budget, should be introduced and should demand additional analytical resources in a period when there is extraordinary pressure to reduce the MoD's running costs and personnel. The initial disparity between aspirations and resources should be alleviated by the diffusion through the MoD and industry of a better understanding of the principles and processes of COEIA, and by the development of computer models to calculate without oversimplification the effects of alterations in key data as a result of development tests or contractual negotiations. But, since the resource-intensive part of a COEIA lies in the formulation of judgements on technical, military and costing issues, rather than in arithmetic, the scale of demand on a limited resource of informed and judicious manpower will continue to present problems.

Another enduring problem is the maintenance of accuracy in forecasting cost and effectiveness. Cost forecasts (whether at system, subsystem, component or resource level) have traditionally relied on the analysis of experience on earlier comparable projects, as a foundation for the judgement of cost analysts. However since the procurement costs of successive new defence equipment projects has grown more rapidly than the defence budget,[3] the frequency of new projects in UK as elsewhere has considerably reduced over recent decades. The RAF, for example, had 27 different types of aircraft enter service in the 1950s (which was admittedly an exceptional decade of rapid technical progress in air systems, and rearmament for the Korean War), 14 in the 1960s, nine in the 1970s, five (including two Tornado variants) in the 1980s, and only two will enter service in the 1990s.[4] This decline in the birth rate of new projects is in sharp contrast to the continuing rapid development in aeronautical technology—notably in the fields of materials, control systems, stealth, software and computer-aided design/manufacture/support. The situation is exacerbated by a parallel trend towards greater variety in MoD procurement. At one time most aircraft projects for the RAF were developed by UK contractors using MoD funding to meet a specified military requirement, so these projects formed a homogeneous database and a sound foundation for cost-forecasting methodology. Lately however many projects have been bought 'off-the-shelf' from foreign suppliers, or have resulted from unique upgrades to earlier projects, or have been developed under a variety of collaborative arrangements with one or more other nations. These later projects have very varied procurement arrangements, and accordingly diverse features, which make cost analysis and forecasting more difficult. Concurrently further complication has been introduced by MoD procurement reforms featuring greater reliance on competition and on fixed-price contracts,[5] and by MoD initiatives to obtain better Reliability and Maintainability (R & M)[6] and to introduce Integrated Logistic Support (ILS) procedures.[7] Each of these (and other) changes, however admirable its aim to achieve better value for money, tends to make increasingly obsolescent MoD's database on the scale and distribution in time of the costs of earlier defence equipment projects, and thus makes it more difficult to use parametric methods to forecast the cost of future projects.

Similarly, forecasting the military effectiveness of new defence equipment must surmount greater difficulties than before the collapse of the Warsaw Pact marked the end of the Cold War. The more-diverse roles envisaged for smaller British forces in the next century demand consideration of a wider range of scenarios, whose topographies and climates are less well established than those of the North German Plain. Operational analysis must also cover a wider range of operations, against different potential enemies and with different possible objectives, which UK Forces might undertake in support of national or international goals. Even if a regrettable outbreak of regional conflicts in the more-fluid international situation following the end of the Cold War has provided some evidence on the military effectiveness of new friendly and hostile defence systems, it will continue to be difficult for analysts to forecast effectiveness in other situations involving troops with different levels of training and motivation.

The difficulties, reviewed in the preceding paragraphs, of forecasting cost and operational effectiveness do not undermine the validity of the COEIA process as a framework for a rational and traceable process of project selection. They do, however, emphasise that COEIA results must be considered with caution and discrimination, and that the key assumptions and methodologies must be illuminated and discussed by the various MoD branches involved.

Notes

1. *Equipment Approvals Committee (EAC), Guidelines for the Dossier System*, Unpublished MoD paper, August 1994.
2. *CIS Cost and Effectiveness: COEIA Guideline* DRA paper DRA/OS/N/CR93011/2.1 dated January 1995.
3. D L I Kirkpatrick and P G Pugh, 'Towards the Starship Enterprise—are current trends in defence costs inexorable?', *Aerospace*, May 1983.
4. Air Marshal Sir Roger Austin, 'Procurement strategies', *Aerospace*, November 1995.
5. *Statement on Defence Estimates Vol. 1*, p.44, (HMSO, London, 1987).
6. NAO *Developments in the Reliability and Maintainability of Defence Equipment*, NAO Report HC690, November 1994.
7. *Integrated Logistic Support*, Defence Standard 00-60.

CHAPTER 10
CONCLUSION

COEIA has sometimes been portrayed as a mechanistic procedure, and as a panacea able to remove all difficulties from defence procurement. *In reality, it is no more than another aid to decision-making in the complex problem of equipment selection,* with additional emphasis on operational analysis and on a wide range of equipment options. Like other approaches, COEIA inputs are derived from and dependent on expert military and technical judgements, and COEIA outputs must be qualified by military factors and procurement uncertainties which are beyond the scope of the most sophisticated battle models and the most rigorous costing methods. Thereafter the final COEIA results must be considered in parallel to other Dossier inputs on financial, industrial, and other national and foreign policy issues in formulating a recommendation for the EAC to select the most attractive equipment option. The outstanding virtue of the COEIA process is that it provides a rational, structured and traceable framework for reviewing the cost and effectiveness of alternative equipment options; as such, it should contribute to better decisions on defence equipment procurement and better values for money from the defence budget.

ANNEX A
LIFE CYCLE COST BREAKDOWN STRUCTURE

There is no ideal breakdown structure which is equally suitable for all types of defence equipment and for all variants of procurement and support strategy, and individual project managers and their contractors may agree to operate on a bespoke breakdown which matches a particular project (provided that it fits the rules of Government accounting). But to provide a common frame of reference and a checklist, the Government/ Industry Life Cycle Cost Policy Committee (LCCPC) has drafted, for consideration by the relevant MoD branches and industry trade associations, the cost breakdown structure shown in Table A1. Those items which are not self explanatory are defined in Table A2.

It should be noted that not all elements of this cost breakdown will be incurred in all projects, and that the distinction between MoD intramural costs and contractors' charges (in the left and right columns of the lowest level elements) is only an accounting convenience (disposal costs, for example, may fall in either category) since both are covered by the MoD budget. It should also be noted that the large costs of supporting defence equipment are normally subdivided between work at 1st line (at the point of operation), 2nd line (away from the point of operation), 3rd line (at a depot), and 4th line (at a contractor's site), and the ratio of MoD costs/ contractors charges may be different in each of these categories.

The life cycle cost breakdown drafted by the LCCPC is a pragmatic structure, based on the mixture of inputs and activities by which the costs of past and current projects have been collected. The breakdown structure will doubtless evolve into an output-based structure as the MoD insists that its own and its contractors' accounting systems are reoriented to provide the cost information necessary to support more-efficient management by budget holders with devolved financial responsibility.

Annex A

Table A1 Components of Life Cycle Cost provided by MoD and *contractors*

ACQUISITION
  RESEARCH AND DEVELOPMENT
    Feasibility Studies
      Technology evaluation   *Technology evaluation Study costs*
    Project Definition
      Technology evaluation   *Technology evaluation Study costs*
    Development
      Govt.- furnished facilities   *Design & Build*
      Govt.-furnished equipment   *Test and evaluation*

  PRODUCTION
    Production investment
      Integrated Logistic Support   *Production facilities and tooling*

      Quality Assurance   *Test equipment*
        Long-lead items
        Production engineering

    System production
      Govt.-furnished equipment   *Manufacture*
        Acceptance tests
        Data

    Demonstration
      Govt.-furnished equipment   *In-service demonstration*
      Govt.-furnished facilities

Choose Your Weapon

Operation investment
    System training   *System training*
                                      Initial spares
                                      Initial munitions
                                      Support equipment
                                      Tools and test equipment
                                      Training equipment
                                      Documentation
                                      Infrastructure

OPERATIONS AND SUPPORT
    OPERATION
        Personnel   *Personnel*
        Fuel and lubricants   *Munitions*
        Transport and Storage   *Transport and storage*
        Continuation Training

    SUPPORT (1ST, 2ND, 3RD, 4TH LINE)
        Personnel   *Personnel*
        Materials   *Materials*
                               Facilities

POST AND CONTINUING DESIGN
        Personnel   *Personnel*
        Equipment/Facilities   *Facilities*

DISPOSAL
        Transport and Storage
        Dismantling
        Destruction and disposal
        Spares recovery
        Sales receipts

Note: All acquisition phases also include costs of MoD project management.

Annex A

TABLE A2 Definitions of Life Cycle Cost Elements

Technology evaluation	The evaluation of new technologies or of novel applications of established technologies
Integrated Logistic Support	Cost of studies to optimise the systems support ability
Acceptance tests	Cost of establishing that the system meets the operator's specification
Data	All publications and data necessary to support system production
Demonstration	Costs of establishing that all contract specifications have been met
Operation investment	Cost of preparing for the system's deployment
Documentation	Costs of preparation and supply of multi-media documentation relating to the system and its support
Infrastructure	Building and other infrastructure necessary for system operation and maintenance
Continuation Training	Training operations and maintenance personnel during the system's service life
Post and Continuing Design	Post Design Services (PDS) and Continuing Design Services (CDS) needed during the system's service life to maintain and enhance its performance respectively
Dismantling	Cost of dismantling defence system in readiness for destruction, sale or recovery of its components
Spares Recovery	Cost of bringing dismantled components into a reusable standard
Sales Receipts	Receipts from the sale of all or part of the defence systems being disposed of

ANNEX B
DISCOUNTING FUTURE EFFECTIVENESS

It is argued in Chapter 8 that military capability, which provides both the security of the homeland and the ability to uphold national interests abroad, has a greater value in the immediate future than many years ahead. This principle is in accordance with the Treasury Technical Guide to Investment Appraisal (cited in Chapter 4) which states that benefits as well as costs should be discounted.

The discount factor to be used may be quantified in terms of the probability p of a war starting in any year of the N-year period considered, and the varying effectiveness E_n of the relevant equipment option against potentially-hostile forces. It may be assumed that future wars will be short relative to time required for the development and production of new equipment, so that future wars must be fought with the equipment which is in service when war begins. It may also be assumed that future wars will be sufficiently infrequent that military equipment used in one war is of negligible value in the next. It follows that the value of military effectiveness in year n is the product of the probability of war recurring in that year and the probability that no war has occurred in the preceding years of the period considered; this product may be written as $p(1-p)^n$. The expected effectiveness of a particular equipment option is the sum of values of the current effectiveness E_n through the period considered, which may be written mathematically as

$$E = pE_0 + p(1-p)E_1 + p(1-p)^2 E_2 \ldots$$

$$\simeq \Sigma_0^N pE_n/(1+p)^n$$

This result is equivalent to discounting future annual values of effectiveness by the probability of war occurring in any future year, which is a similar process to the approved IA procedure of discounting the expenditure which falls in future years (see Chapter 4). It follows that in periods

Annex B

of international tension when p is perceived to be high (as in the years preceding both World Wars) this discounting procedure would bias equipment selection more strongly towards options which could enter service sooner rather than later.

The probability p must always be a subjective value, derived from diplomatic and military judgement. It is indicative, however, that in the last century, the UK has been involved in two general (or World) wars and four regional wars (Boer, Korean, Falklands, Gulf). It follows that if only general wars were considered, the average historical value of p would be two per cent, but if regional wars are also included p would be six per cent. This procedure would be more complex if the perceived value of p varied in future years—for example under a Ten Year Rule assuming that there will be no war for the next 10 years, p would be set at zero for those years. It will always be difficult to agree the appropriate value (or values) for p, but since it is most unlikely to be zero into the infinite future, it is arguable that some discounting of effectiveness may be appropriate.